NATIONAL GEOGRAPHIC

Shadow Play

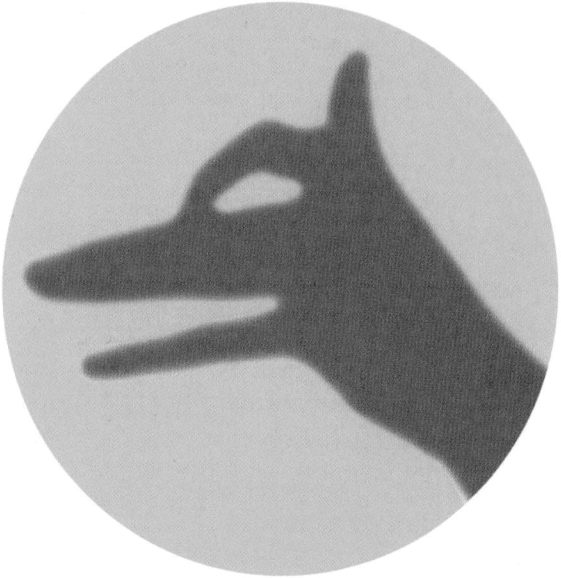

Helen Mammides

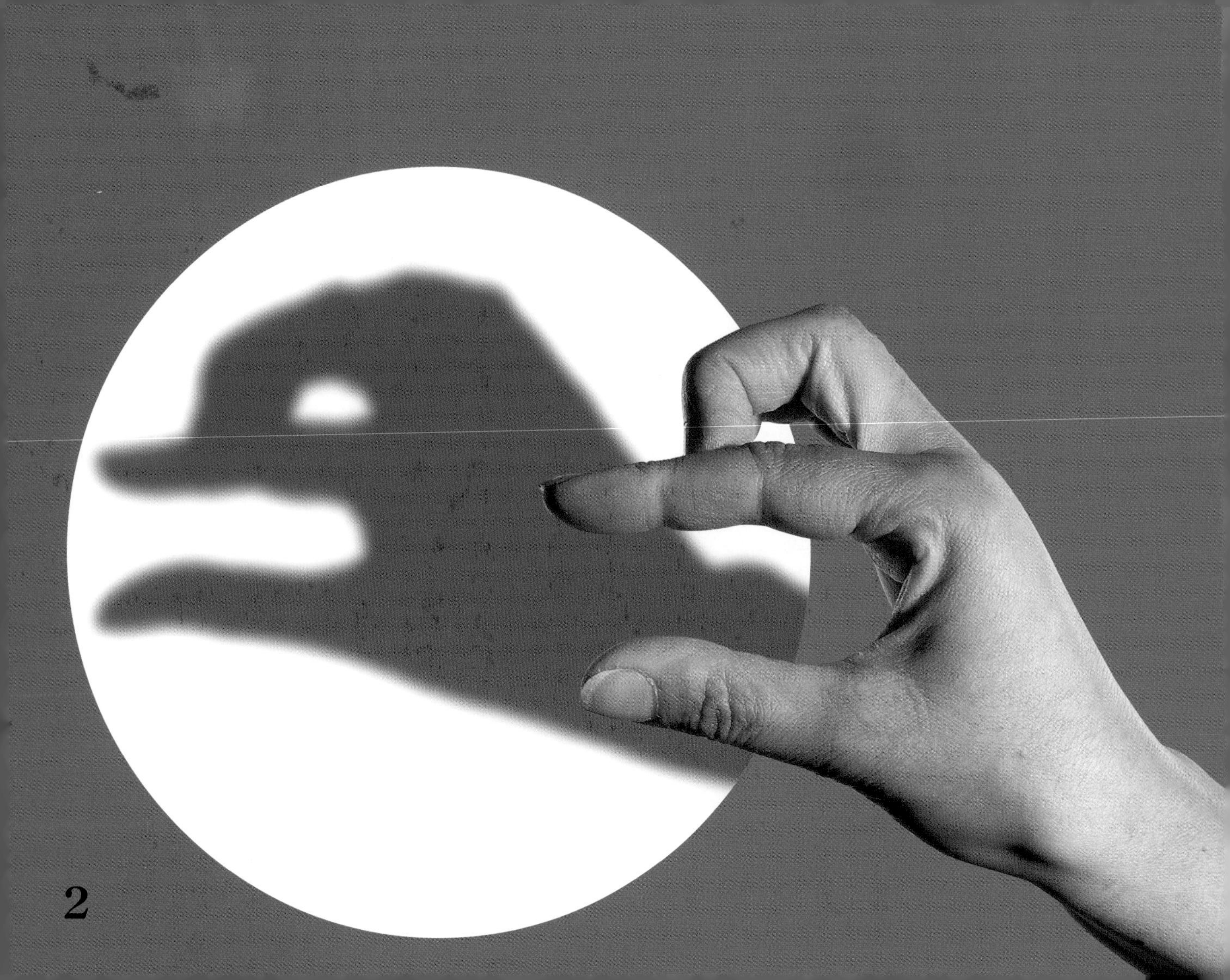

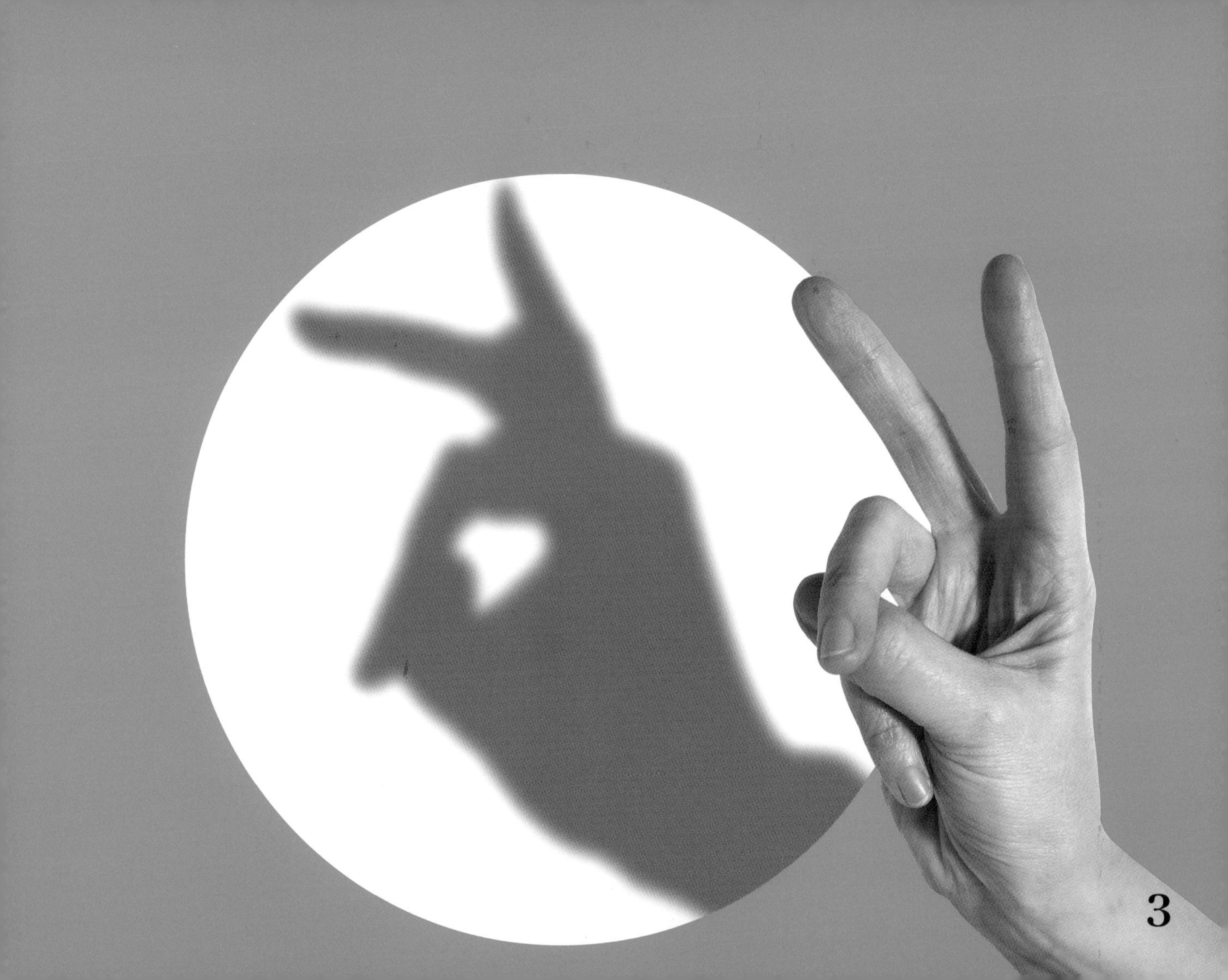

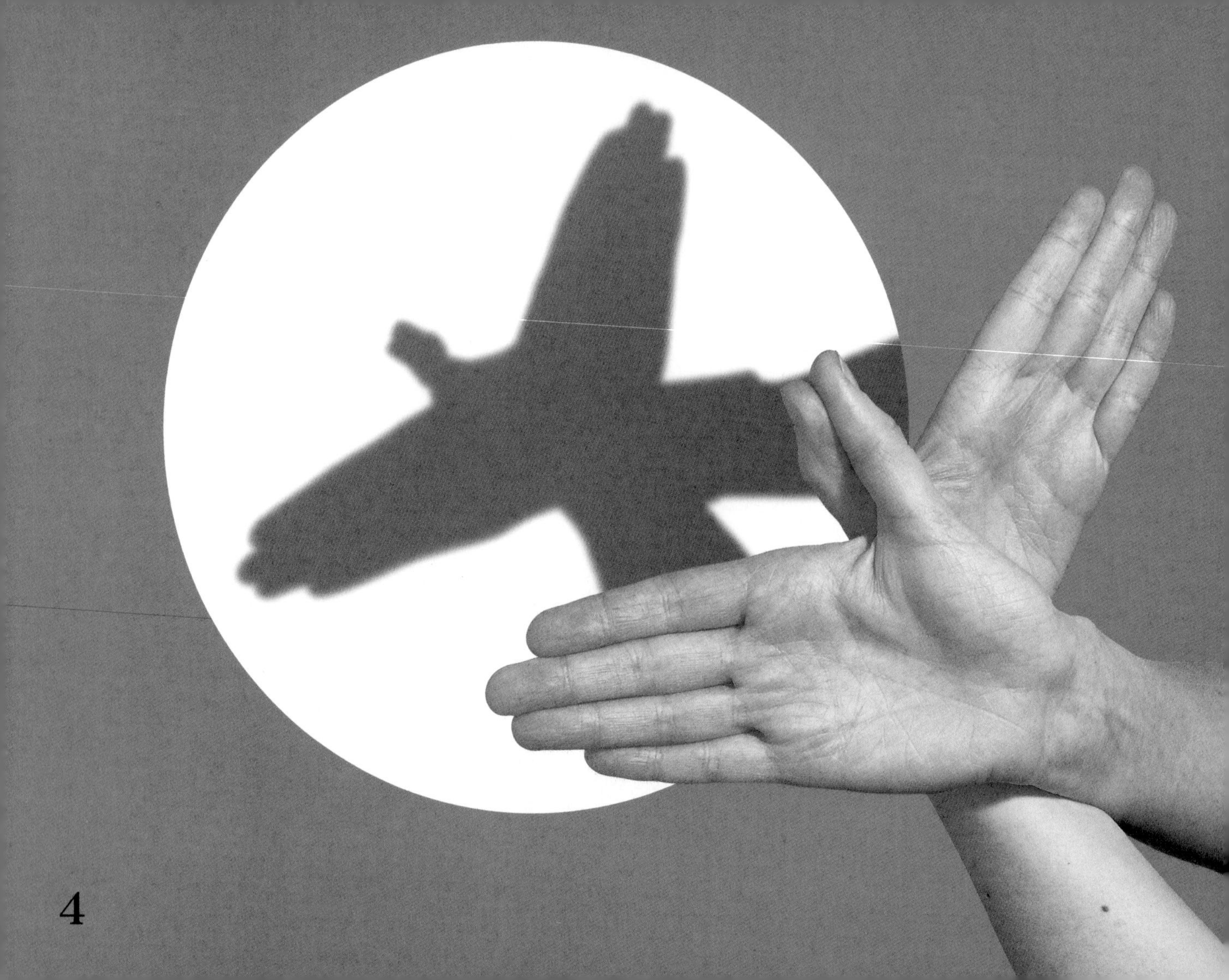

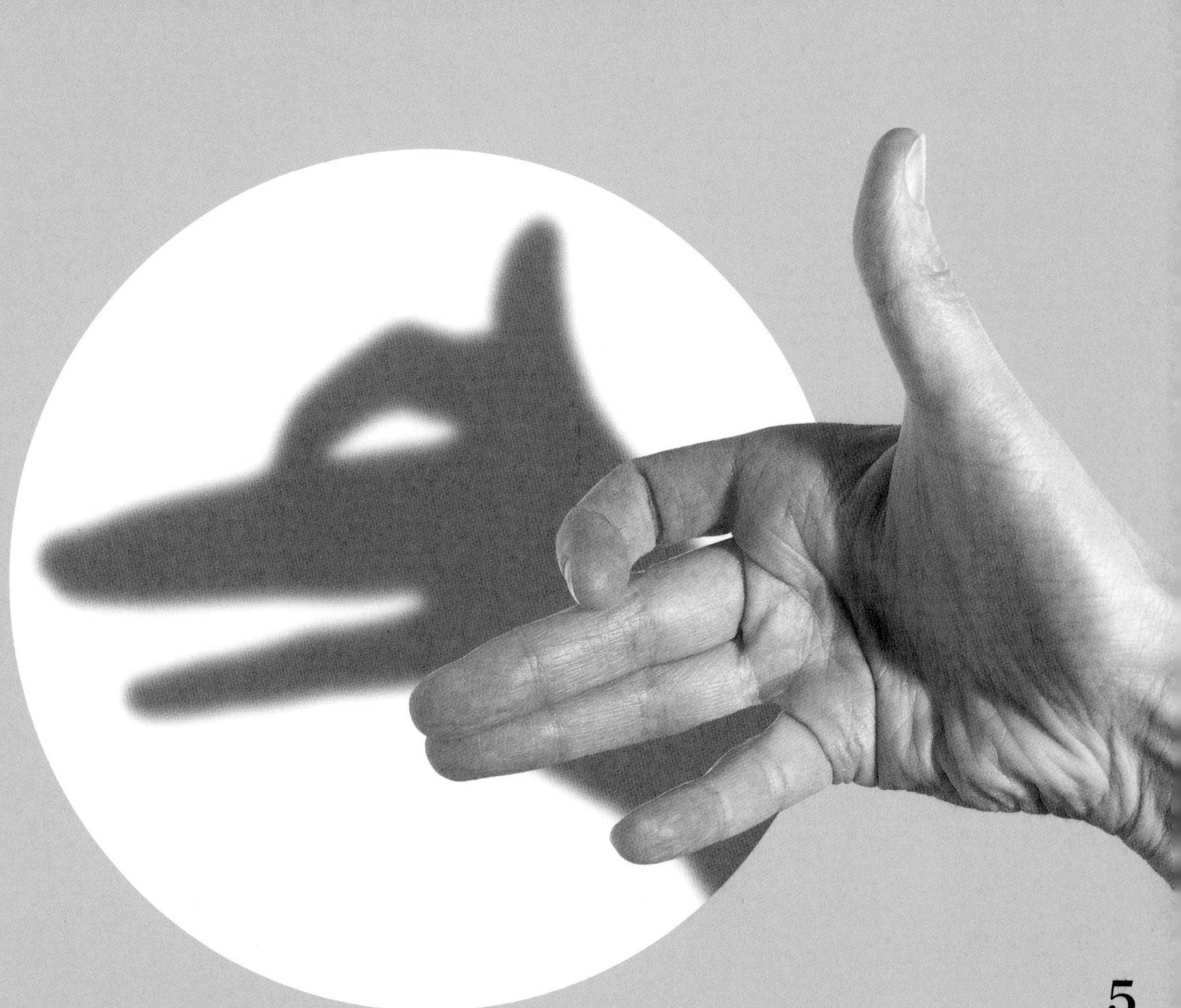

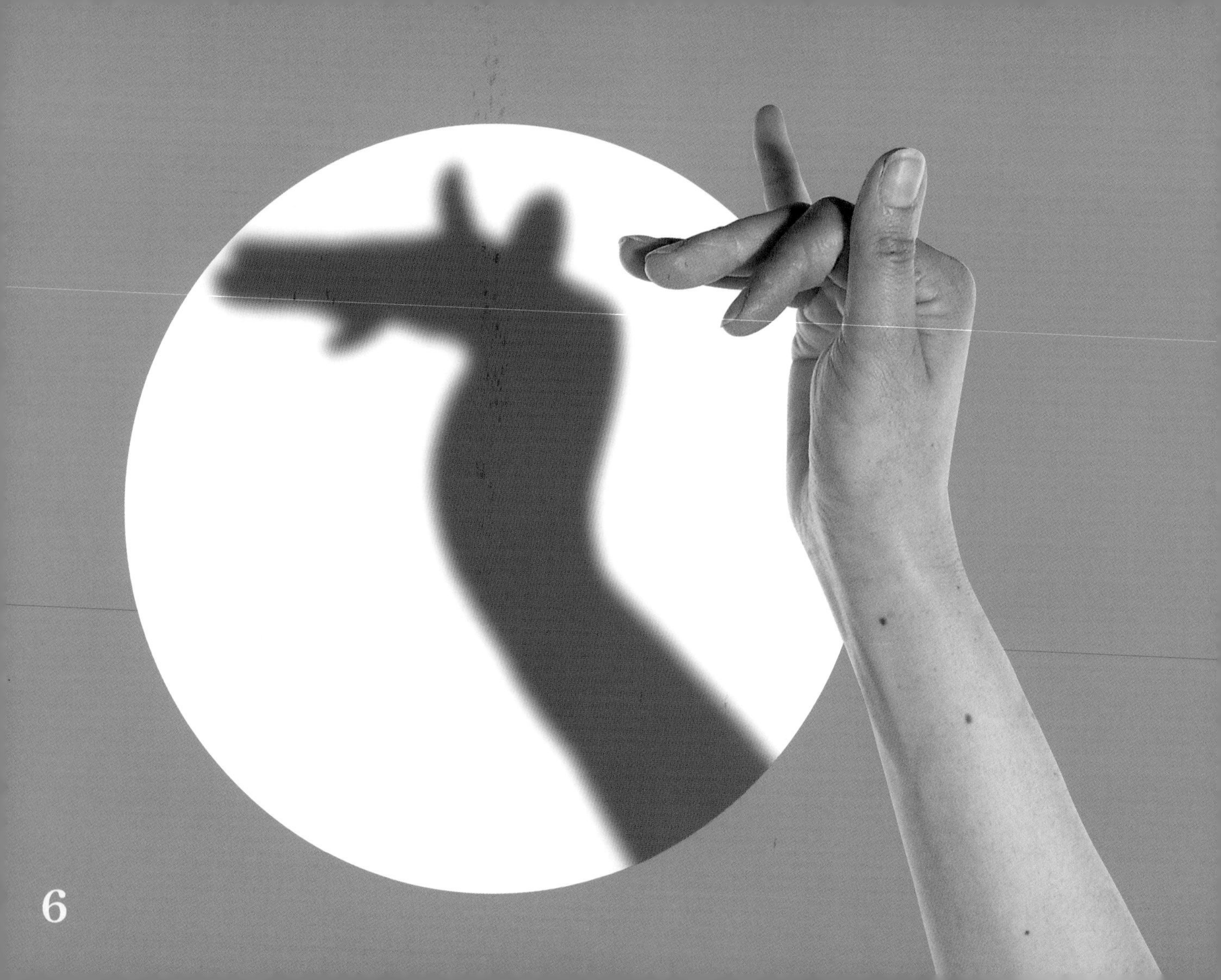

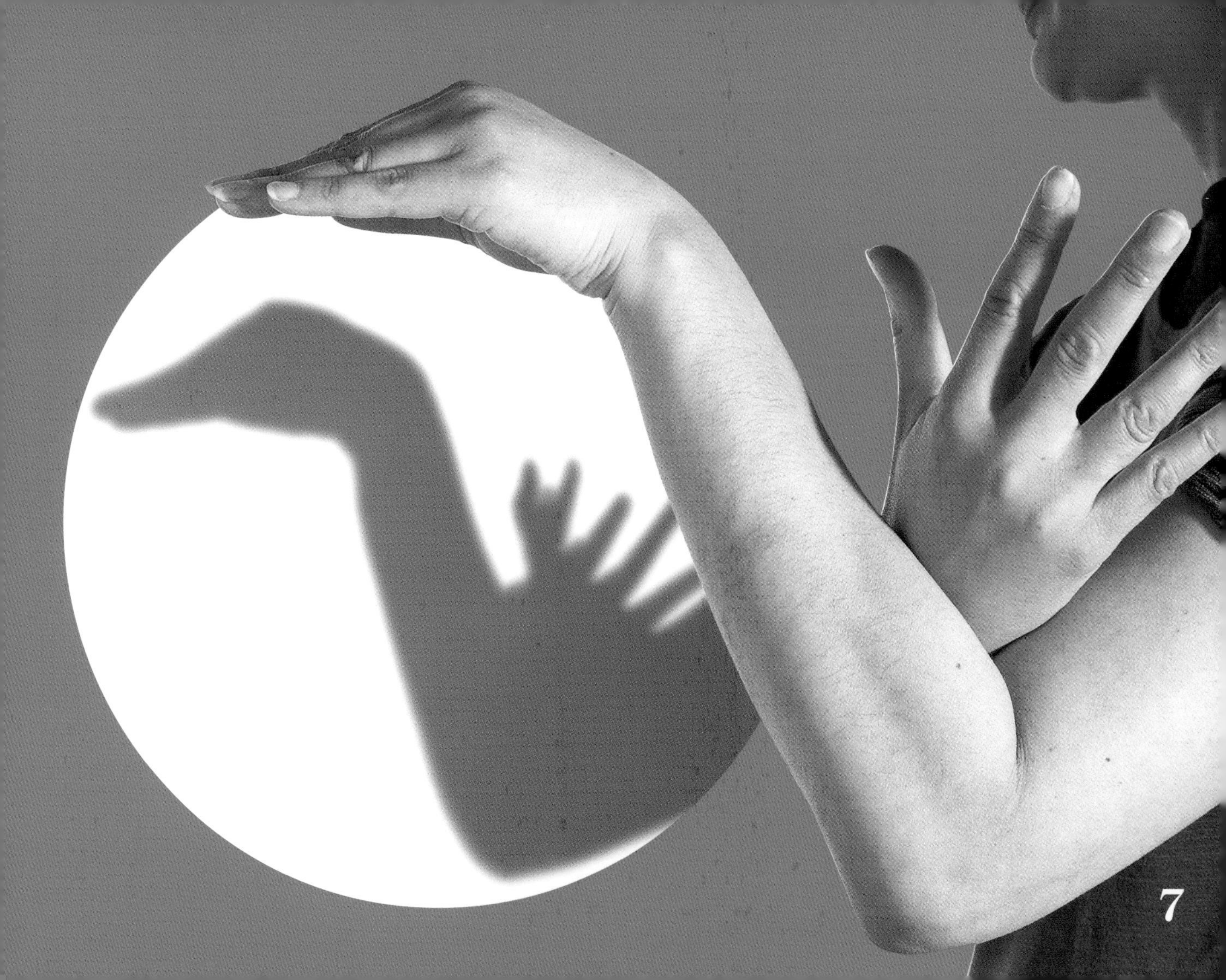

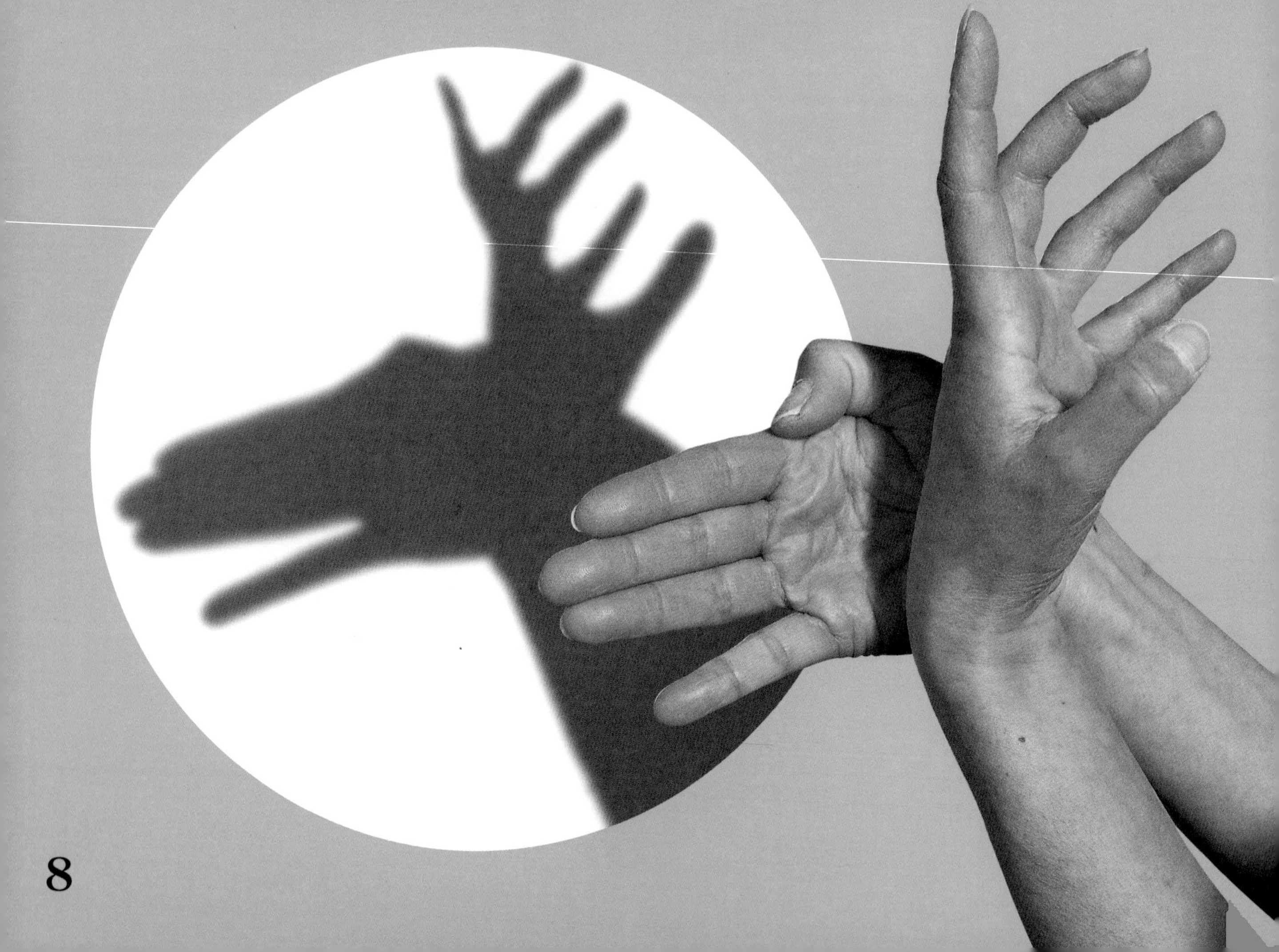